CHRISTOPHER COLUMBUS

By Michael Rajczak

Gareth Stevens

Library of Congress Cataloging-in-Publication Data

Rajczak, Michael.
 Christopher Columbus / Michael Rajczak.
     pages cm. — (What you didn't know about history)
 Includes index.
ISBN 978-1-4824-1946-7 (pbk.)
ISBN 978-1-4824-1945-0 (6 pack)
ISBN 978-1-4824-1947-4 (library binding)
1. Columbus, Christopher—Juvenile literature. 2. Explorers—America—Biography—Juvenile literature. 3. Explorers—Spain—Biography—Juvenile literature. 4. America—Discovery and exploration—Spanish—Juvenile literature. I. Title.
E111.R2135 2015
970.01'5092—dc23
 [B]
                                        2014034321

First Edition

Published in 2015 by
Gareth Stevens Publishing
111 East 14th Street, Suite 349
New York, NY 10003

Copyright © 2015 Gareth Stevens Publishing

Designer: Andrea Davison-Bartolotta
Editor: Kristen Rajczak

Photo credits: Cover, p. 1 Leemage/Universal Images Group/Getty Images; p. 5 Toni Genes/Shutterstock.com; p. 6 Peter Dennis/Thinkstock; p. 7 Duncan Walker/E+/Getty Images; p. 9 Culture Club/Hulton Archive/Getty Images; p. 10 TonyBaggett/iStock/Thinkstock; p. 11 LTL/Hulton Fine Art Collection/UIG/Getty Images; p. 13 Kean Collection/Getty Images; p. 15 (inset) Richard Schlecht/National Geographic/Getty Images; p. 15 (main) ekler/Shutterstock.com; p. 17 Martin Waldseemüller/LOC.gov; p. 19 Mondadori Portfolio/Hulton Fine Art Collection/Getty Images; p. 20 Georgios Kollidas/Shutterstock.com; p. 21 Phirosiberia/Wikimedia Commons.

Printed in the United States of America

CPSIA compliance information: Batch #CW15GS: For further information contact Gareth Stevens, New York, New York at 1-800-542-2595.

CONTENTS

Words in the glossary appear in **bold** type the first time they are used in the text.

The real name of one of the most well-known explorers in history isn't commonly in history books. We know him by the English **version** of his name: Christopher Columbus. Born in Italy, his name in Italian was Cristoforo Colombo. When he lived in Spain later in life, he changed his name to Cristóbal Colón!

No matter what you call him, history shows that Christopher Columbus's **voyages** turned out to be very important to the **exploration** of the Western **Hemisphere**—even though he thought he was in Asia!

Did You Know?

It's a **myth** that Christopher wanted to prove Earth was round. The ancient Greeks were likely the first to realize Earth's shape. By Christopher's time, many people knew it.

Christopher's birth name is sometimes reported as Christoffa Corombo.

Christopher was most likely born in 1451 in Genoa, a city in what is now northwest Italy. However, Portugal, Greece, Corsica, and other places have tried to claim that Christopher was born there, not Genoa.

Christopher's father was a wool worker and weaver. Christopher worked with his father until he was a teenager and probably didn't go to school. Genoa was a seaport and center of trade. Christopher became interested in the ships he saw come in. Like many boys from Genoa, he soon went to sea.

Did You Know?

As an adult, Christopher could read and write, and he spoke several languages, including Portuguese and some Latin.

Not much else is known about Christopher's early life. Historians do know that by 1470, Christopher had already begun making his living at sea.

LUCKY SHIPWRECK

In 1476, Christopher survived a shipwreck off the coast of Portugal! After finding his way ashore, Christopher stayed there and lived in Portugal's capital city of Lisbon. The shipwreck was somewhat lucky. Portugal was the best place to find good ships and the latest knowledge about exploration.

Christopher married Felipa Moniz Perestrelo in 1479. Her father introduced Christopher to charts, maps, and reports of Atlantic voyages. It was about this time that Christopher began planning to sail west.

Did You Know?

During the 1400s, Portugal was exploring the west coast of Africa. Their discoveries and colonies would become the beginnings of the African slave trade.

Christopher sailed to Iceland, Ireland, and the island of Madeira with the Portuguese before he began preparing to sail to the uncharted west.

Christopher planned to sail westward from Europe and find a quicker trade **route** to Asia. At the time, Asian goods like spices and silks were worth a lot in Europe. King John II of Portugal **rejected** the idea.

Christopher's wife died in 1485. He left Portugal for Spain where he would again look for support for his voyage. King Ferdinand II and Queen Isabella I, rulers of the two biggest kingdoms in Spain, rejected Christopher at first. They eventually agreed to his plan.

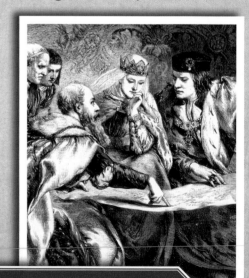

Did You Know?

Christopher was supposed to receive 10 percent of the money earned from his voyage. Since Ferdinand and Isabella thought he would never return, they agreed to the deal.

Christopher was turned down in Portugal because King John II's advisers said Christopher's journey would take much longer than he thought.

ALMOST TURNED BACK

Columbus set sail from Spain on August 3, 1492, with three ships: the *Santa Clara*, the *Pinta*, and the *Santa Maria*.

The journey across the Atlantic took more than a month. Christopher kept the true distance they traveled from his crew. He thought they'd be afraid if they knew the truth. Still, by October, the crew worried they were lost and had too few supplies for the return trip. Christopher said if they didn't see land in 2 days, they would turn back. They saw land the next day.

Did You Know?

The *Santa Clara*'s nickname was the *Niña* after the man who owned it. It and the *Pinta* were small ships called caravels. The *Santa Maria* was a large ship used to carry goods.

Christopher and his crew sailed to the Canary Islands before continuing their journey across the Atlantic to take advantage of the good sailing winds in that part of the ocean.

13

WHERE DID HE LAND?

No one is sure exactly where Christopher first came ashore in the Americas. It was likely an island in the Bahamas, but which one is unknown. Others say it was one of the islands farther south, such as Grand Turk. Christopher named this first island San Salvador. Whether it's the island now called San Salvador, no one knows.

Christopher spent a few days visiting small islands. Then, he moved on to exploring the larger islands of Cuba and Hispaniola.

Did You Know?

Another myth says Christopher discovered the Americas. However, **nomads** from Asia crossed a land bridge to North America about 15,000 years ago. In addition, Leif Erikson and his Viking crew reached Canada around the year 1000.

Though it's not known exactly where Christopher's ships landed first, historians do know he later found a lot of gold.

Bahamas

Cuba

Hispaniola

the *Santa Maria* ran aground off Hispaniola

DISAPPOINTMENTS

Christopher believed he had reached islands just east of Asia. However, it was clear that he hadn't found a quicker trade route to China. He didn't find the Chinese cities and goods other explorers had. That made his voyage seem like a failure. He didn't know he had found new land.

In addition, his largest ship—the *Santa Maria*—was destroyed. He had to leave about 40 men behind when he sailed back to Spain in January 1493.

Did You Know?

Christopher would claim he had been close to Asia until he died. He tried to make others believe Earth was shaped like a pear so his ideas made sense!

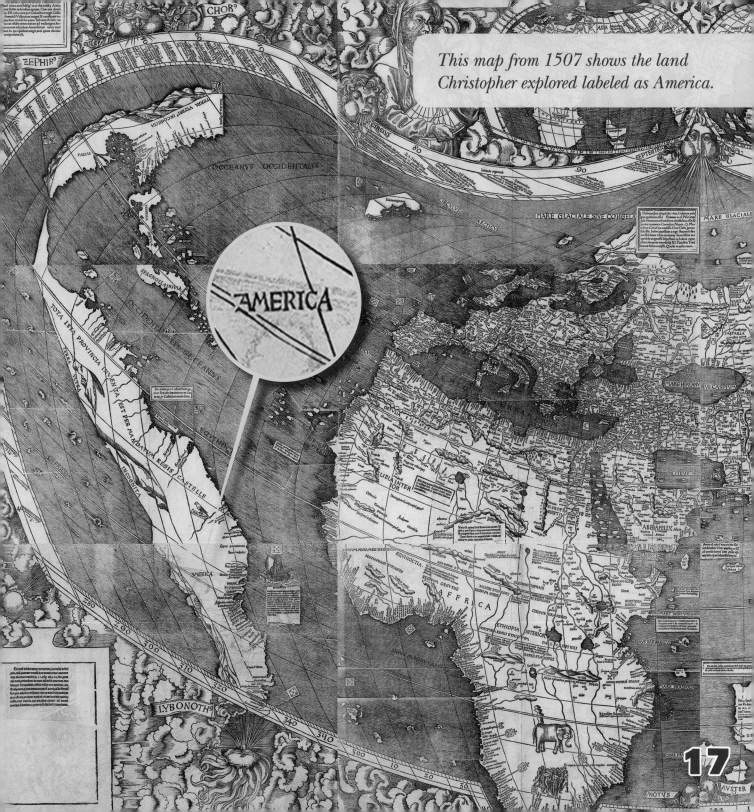

This map from 1507 shows the land Christopher explored labeled as America.

NOT A HAPPY ENDING

Even though Christopher didn't fulfill his promise of finding a trade route, he was still able to get funding, or money, for more voyages across the Atlantic. In fact, he was able to make three more voyages! Christopher explored more around the Caribbean islands, Central America, and South America.

One of his greatest discoveries was the native people living there. However, Christopher treated them **brutally**, even enslaving some. Christopher acted so badly, he was taken back to Spain in chains and imprisoned in 1500.

Did You Know?

In 1504, Christopher was **stranded** in Jamaica. The natives wouldn't help him. Remembering that a **lunar eclipse** was due, he said they had angered his god. When a red moon rose, they became fearful and agreed to help.

Christopher had been the governor of the new lands he explored. He lost his title after his imprisonment—but was still granted money for a fourth voyage!

*L*EGACY

The rulers of Spain didn't pay Christopher fairly for his voyages. Aging and sickly, Columbus continued to ask King Ferdinand for his promised wealth. Christopher died in 1506 at age 54. His family never received what was owed.

News of Christopher's discoveries caused great excitement throughout Europe. Other nations sent explorers and created settlements in the Americas partly because of Christopher's voyages. Although he didn't really discover America, his travels across the Atlantic helped open it up for the rest of Europe.

Did You Know?

Many cities, schools, and counties are named in honor of Christopher Columbus, including Columbia University; Columbus, Ohio; and the District of Columbia.

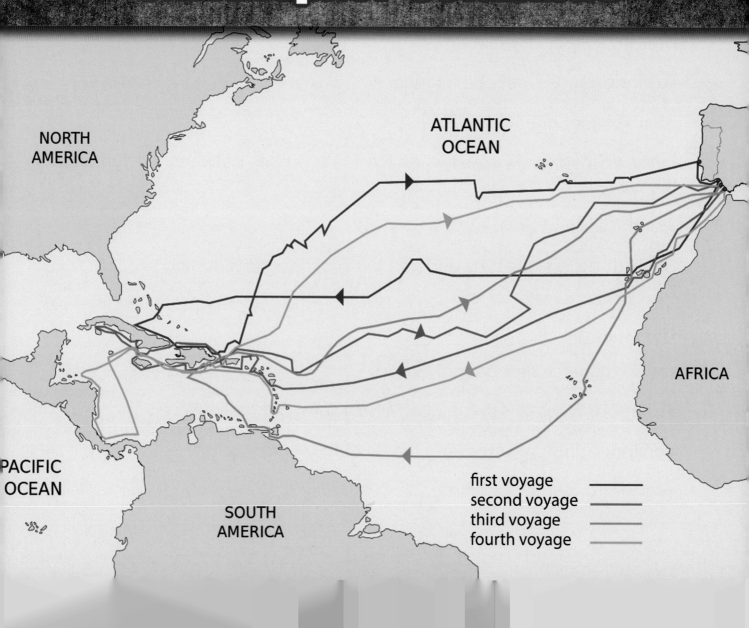

The Voyages of Christopher Columbus

NORTH AMERICA

ATLANTIC OCEAN

AFRICA

PACIFIC OCEAN

SOUTH AMERICA

first voyage
second voyage
third voyage
fourth voyage

LOSSARY

brutally: especially mean

exploration: the act of exploring

hemisphere: one half of Earth

lunar eclipse: a sky event when the Earth passes between the sun and the moon

myth: a legend or story

nomad: a person who wanders from place to place to find shelter and food

reject: to refuse

route: a course that people travel

stranded: to be left in a place without a way to leave it

version: a form of something that is different from others

voyage: a journey by ship

FOR MORE INFORMATION

Books

Bader, Bonnie. *Who Was Christopher Columbus?* New York, NY: Grosset & Dunlap, 2013.

Macdonald, Fiona. *You Wouldn't Want to Sail with Christopher Columbus! Uncharted Waters You'd Rather Not Cross.* New York, NY: Franklin Watts, 2014.

Websites

Christopher Columbus Biography for Kids
mrnussbaum.com/columbus/
Discover more facts and watch a video about Columbus.

World Explorers
www.ducksters.com/biography/explorers/
Read about many other explorers here.

Index